THE 15 WALKS WITH 15 FURT

Walk Number	Start Point - see back cover map	Miles	Type of Terrain	Average Time	
1	Painswick Beacon	6½	M/H	3¾ hours	
option 2	as above	4	M/H	2¼ hours	
option 3	Cranham Church	4½	M/H	2¾ hours	
2	Painswick Walkers' CP	5¾	M	3 hours	striking views, common, streams
3	Shortwood	3½	M	1¾ hours	topograph, park and woodland
option 2	as above	1¾	L	1 hour	easy walking to hill fort, views
option 3	as above	5	M	2½ hours	combination of the above two
4	near Miserden	5¼	M	3 hours	varied countryside, Misarden Park
option 2	as above	4¼	M	2¼ hours	shorter version of the above route
option 3	Bisley or Miserden	10½	M	5¾ hours	Walk 4 and Walk 5
5	Bisley	5	M	2¾ hours	solitude, deep valleys, villages
6	near Eastington	4½	L	2¼ hours	historical village, canal and river
7	Cowcombe Hill	4	M	2 hours	hillside, pretty Golden Valley
option 2	as above	5	M	2½ hours	as above with extra canal loop
8	Minchinhampton	7	M/H	3½ hours	National Trust commons, views
9	Minchinhampton	7½	M	3¾ hours	open hillside, pond, views
option 2	Hampton Fields	3	M	1½ hours	shorter version of above route
option 3	Minchinhampton	14½	M/H	7½ hours	Walk 8 and Walk 9
10	Stinchcombe Hill	4	M/H	2½ hours	open hillside, village, meadows
option 2	as above	2	L	1 hour	tour of hilltop, superb views
option 3	as above	6	M/H	3½ hours	combination of above two
11	Cam Peak (or Coaley Peak)	7½	H	4½ hours	outlier Cotswold Hills and a section of the Cotswold Way
option 2	Cam Peak	3¾	H	2¼ hours	outlier hills, Uley Bury, views
12	Owlpen	5	M/H	3 hours	hill fort, villages, excellent views
option 2	Owlpen/Cam Peak	12½	H	7 hours	Walk 11 and Walk 12
option 3	as above	8¾	H	4½ hours	Walk 11 option 2 and Walk 12
13	Wotton-under-Edge	6	M	3 hours	woods, open views, historic town
14	Beverston Castle	5½	L/M	2¾ hours	fields, woods, Chavenage House
option 2	as above	3	L	1½ hours	just one stile, open fields, views
15	Wortley	5	M	2½ hours	deep bottoms, hilltop village, views

Type of Terrain

L   Level or little climbing   No walk is completely level in this scenic area.

M   Moderate   Some hills which may be steep at times, but many easier sections too.

H   Hilly   Up and down for much of the time, but with views to compensate.

Average Time

We have shown average times. You will need to allow more time for a picnic or pub lunch, for taking it easy and/or stopping to enjoy the views, or conversely you will take less time if you like walking quickly.

- **DESCRIPTION:** This fairly hilly 6½ mile walk (10½ km) (3¾ hours) drops down from near Painswick Beacon into the valley then up through Ebworth beechwoods, returning by Cranham Common, with views and later the Cotswold Way passing Iron Age Fort and Painswick Beacon.
- **OPTION 2 WEST:** Fairly hilly 4 miles (6.5 km) (2¼ hours) - cut along stream (points ABEFA).
- **OPTION 3 EAST:** Fairly hilly 4½ miles (7 km) (2¾ hrs) - (points DEBCD). From Cranham.
- **DIRECTIONS:** From Gloucester take B4073. Turn left signed Painswick Beacon. From Stroud or Cheltenham turn off A46 at sign to Painswick Beacon. **PARK** by Catbrain Quarry millstone (do not block entrance) or just over the brow, grid reference 867 116, OS maps Landranger 162 and 163, Explorer 179. **ALTERNATIVE AND OPTION 3 START** Near Cranham Church. From A46 to Cranham, right at X-roads, ½ mile to park by church, grid ref. 891 124, by school on Sunday.
- **BUS:** No 46 from Cheltenham or Stroud to Paradise. Hourly, four return trips on Sundays.
- **FOOD & DRINK:** Royal William on the A46 near Cranham, (01452 813650), Black Horse, Cranham (½ mile off route) (01452 812217).

[A]   Start by millstone outside quarry and look for finger post to take lower path (part of Wysis Way) through wood to A46. Turn sharp left to cross road CAREFULLY to bus stop and go along pavement passing former *Adam and Eve* pub in Paradise (hanging sign frame still there), then down steps and through hedge into garden QUIETLY bearing left to stile into field. Turn right passing gardens then left steeply down field to a gate / stile. Cross stream, looking out for wild daffodils in spring. Go through gate into wood, over stile on right and into meadow over stile. Cross field dropping down to gate / stile then another stile on right into an often muddy farmyard. Go straight across between the barns, over stile and turn left. Soon cross another stile to right of gate passing the classical Cotswold front of Damsells Farmhouse, bearing left across drive to a stile at the wall end. Then go up field and down to a stile / gate, turn right down fence into track and through gate to pass a cottage on left. **MAIN WALK** This turns right through metal gate. [**OPTION 2, WEST link, see page 3.**]

[B]   [**OPTION 3 rejoins.**] Follow field edge up past barn ignoring gate. Later go through gate, up field and through gate out onto road. Turn right signed Sheepscombe, then left through gate up drive / garden of *Trench Hill*, out via a gate following power line to a stile / gate into Lord's and Lady's Woods. Now go upwards, crossing a track to top then veering right with wall on left.

Follow track, looking for Sheepscombe (Laurie Lee's) cricket ground through trees on right, and come to gate with old stile on right. Enter part of the Cotswold Commons and Beechwoods National Nature Reserve where access is restricted to waymarked paths only. Go through gate and keep to left around Ebworth Plantation edge until path bears up steeply off track and turns left to lead into the *Old Ebworth Centre*. Look back along track to carving *Spirit of the Woods. The Centre was created from 17th century Cotswold farm buildings, now*

In Paradise

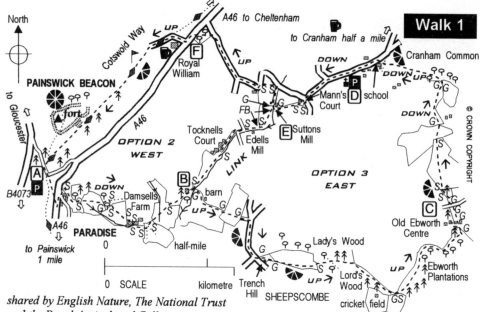

shared by English Nature, The National Trust and the Royal Agricultural College.

[C]   After leaving Centre carry on up field through two gates, wall on left, over stile into wood (full of wild garlic in spring). Then over stile and across middle of large field with fine views over Cranham Woods. Go down over stile and through gateway to bottom of valley, crossing small stream on right. Turn left through gates onto lovely uphill track in wood leading on to Cranham Common and amazing views. Keep straight on down, leaving the common by a house called *Picardy*, meeting the road by the school. Turn left near school onto road, to reach Cranham Church *where lie the ashes of Colonel Carne of the Glosters, awarded the VC following the Korean War.*

[D]   [ALTERNATIVE START] Walk from Cranham Church (or school on Sundays) down road forking left to *Mann's Court*. Go over old stone stile and QUIETLY through garden using ingenious sliding rails. Follow right field edge down through gate into paddock, to reach stream. [Option 3, EAST link, see next column.]

[E]   [OPTION 2 rejoins.] Route goes through wicket gate, passing mill buildings *(Suttons Mill)* and along drive to road. Go over stile on left, and climb following power line to stile. Look for good views behind to Cranham

Common and Church. Go left up road and when within 100 yards of A46 cut through woods to cross the A46 CAREFULLY to the Royal William.

[F]   Go up road on right to the waymarked Cotswold Way (page 32). Follow across golf course watching for stray shots and by edge of hill fort. If time permits before finishing the walk a diversion to the Beacon will often be rewarded with fine views of the Severn Vale.

[OPTION 2 WEST - link directions. Go over stile ahead by wooden gate (often muddy) to follow valley with stream on right. Bear left after stile near *Tocknells Court* to go along drive. Cross road, over stile passing mill to footbridge on right. Go up and left by pond to stile, half left up field and across to footbridge on right. Go left to wicket gate to rejoin main walk at E.]

[OPTION 3 EAST - link directions. Bear left over footbridge and left along stream side. Bear slightly away from stream and rejoin in a short while. Cross stile to pass by old mill pond and bear right to footbridge. Bear left to pass Mill and go to stile to road. Cross and go along *Tocknells Court* drive to cattle grid. Go left to stile and by stream to further stile. Turn left to metal gate to rejoin the full walk at B.]

3

Walk 2
5¾ miles

Painswick, Huddinknoll Hill and Edge Common
Harold and Betty Wood

- **DESCRIPTION:** A moderately hilly 5¾ mile (10 km) (3 hours) Cotswold walk. A mix of farm footpaths, tracks and lanes. Beautiful views in all directions - it is rewarding to look behind you now and again. From the escarpment on a clear day views can be obtained as far as the Brecon Beacons. If you have not visited Painswick before allow plenty of time to enjoy this delightful place. There is a visitors' pay/display car park near Church in Stamages Lane for after the walk.
- **DIRECTIONS:** From Cheltenham or Stroud, use A46, turn at Painswick traffic lights uphill on B4073 towards Gloucester. Turn right into Golf Course Road after half a mile. From Gloucester take the B4073. When nearing Painswick, in wood, turn left at Golf Course Road (just after entrance to Painswick House Rococo Gardens on right. **PARK** in free walkers'/ramblers' car park on left of Golf Course Road, grid reference 866 104, OS maps Landranger 162 or Explorer 179.
- **BY BUS** to Painswick from Stroud, Cheltenham and Gloucester. A limited Sunday service runs from Stroud and Cheltenham. From main road, go up Gloucester Street, turn left at Butt Green.
- **FOOD & DRINK:** Royal Oak Inn, Painswick (01452 813129), Chancellors Tea-Rooms, Painswick (01452 812451) and the Edgemoor Inn (01452 813576).

[A]   Leave car park and walk back to main road. Turn left downhill for ¼ mile. After passing a telephone box turn sharp right into Butt Green (cul-de-sac). At end turn left and immediately right onto footpath with cottages on your right. Now go over stile and follow path down. On the right are the grounds of

Painswick House, and you should have fine views of the house. Follow this boundary over two more stiles and through a gateway, then up and down to a stile by gate near small stream. Keep to right uphill over stone stile into farm drive.

[B]   Go through gate opposite and cross corner of field on similar line to stile ahead. Cross and follow hedge, now on your right, in the same direction. Just after passing small

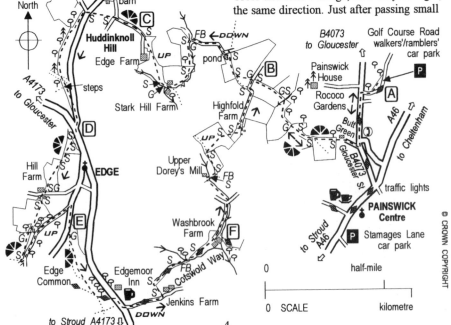

4

pond on left, climb stile into sunken path, and ignoring stile opposite, go left down damp sloping path. Bear left at the bottom over a bridge and by gate, over stile and follow stream on left. Go over stile into a light wood and after holly grove ignore bridge on left to go forward QUIETLY through left side of a fine garden with fish pool on your right. Go through a gate by cattle grid, across drive to enclosed path leading to stile. Climb hilly field, keeping right of Edge Farm to top corner and concealed stile into road. Turn right and walk up road. Look for fine view of Painswick Beacon on right and Church behind you.

C Where road bears right go ahead by a pinch stile and cross a field with modernised barn on right to stone stile. Cross the road and go diagonally up bank on bridleway which becomes wider with railing on right. *Good views on right to Severn Vale, Forest of Dean and the Brecon Beacons.* A hundred yards after the track is crossed by two rails you may see a metal kissing gate and steps downhill on right. Do not go down, but notice passing places on steps - for ladies in crinoline dresses! Go to end of track bearing right onto road which joins busy A4173.

Painswick House with Rococo Gardens

D After 20 yards uphill cross CAREFULLY to stile then down steps over stile into a field. Walk half left to cross a stile in corner. Here are more views, including May Hill with its trees. Follow hedge on right and after 50 yards cross stile on right into large meadow. Bear left to cross stile by gate in far corner of field beside house. In road turn right and immediately left over stile and along enclosed path. After 50 yards cross stile into large field. Head half left to corner of wood but do NOT cross into it. The route now heads along the broad track under trees to a gate. Go slightly up in next

field on same line and after 100 yards look behind for a magnificent view of the Malverns. At far left end of field go over stile, hidden at first. Turn left up road for nearly 600 yards to main road. At junction turn sharp right with CARE. After 100 yards on left enter common through the right of two large wooden gates.

E Take the path ahead and follow this across delightful Edge Common (also known as Rudge Hill). There are several paths across the common all leading in a similar direction, so follow one of them. In a few minutes make your way down to the road near to the Edgemoor Inn. You may spot the Cotswold Way *(see page 32)* joining from right. Now cross the busy A4173 with CARE to Jenkins Lane (Edgemoor Inn is on your left). After 250 yards down road, turn left through stone pinch stile. Soon cross stile on right by white circular target and muddy track. Go down field to right corner and into wood. Go down steps, over bridge and through wood to a stile. Go over and in 100 yards go over a stile on the left on to a track, following it right.

F At junction by Washbrook farmhouse where Cotswold Way turns right, keep straight on up drive. Cross a road into Upper Dorey's Mill Lane to reach mill house at the end. QUIETLY cross parking area just before the house. Turn RIGHT down through the garden with a small pond on your left over a bridge and stile. Follow path steeply up to stile at top. Go over and then left over stile through one field to another stile. Cross and turn right heading for farm buildings up hill. Cross two further stiles and continue up farm drive. Soon after double bend turn right over the stone slab stile to retrace your route.

5

- **DESCRIPTION:** This moderate 3½ mile (5½ km) (1¾ hours) walk initially follows the Cotswold Way on National Trust land over open country to the topograph from where there are excellent and wide ranging views over the Severn Vale, and on a clear day the unmistakeable May Hill with its clump of trees, Forest of Dean, and Severn Bridge and Second Severn Crossing. The route goes down in the valley and along a quiet road to Standish Park Farm Estate, before climbing to Standish Wood, belonging to the National Trust. The 1½ mile long path undulates gently through the lovely woods, with a fairly steep section shortly before the end of the walk.
- **OPTION 2:** easy 1¾ miles (3 km) (1 hour) - a there-and-back stroll to Haresfield Beacon, where there are more excellent views.
- **OPTION 3:** moderate 5 miles (8 km) (2½ hours) - include stroll to Beacon before main route.
- **DIRECTIONS:** From the east, turn off the A4173 at Edge Church to junction X on map (grid reference 838 086). From the south, take the unclassified road from Stroud up through Whiteshill to junction X. From X go along side road towards Haresfield Beacon for about half a mile. **PARK** in Shortwood, National Trust Cripplegate car park, grid reference 832 086, OS maps Landranger 162 or Explorer 179.
- **BY BUS:** Mon-Sat hourly Stroud/Gloucester 93 to Haresfield Beacon turn point X. Start ½ mile.
- **FOOD & DRINK:** Edgemoor Inn (01452 813576), ¾ mile south of Edge Church on A4173, or Woodcutters Arms, Whiteshill (01453 764870), on unclassified road to Stroud.

[A] **MAIN WALK** Leave the car park by a timber gate adjacent to a NT stone structure. Proceed ahead across open grassland slightly to right of a clump of trees, just over 100 yards away. At that point you will probably be able to see the topograph, 400 yards further on. *This topograph was built in 1934, and points to many places of interest, although it predates the two Severn bridges and nuclear power stations at Oldbury and Berkeley (the latter now closed).*

[B] From the topograph ignore the path ahead and turn left towards a grass track, then right to follow the track downhill, with large bushes on the left, until you come to a stile in the right hand corner of a field at a fence junction. Cross the stile where there is a bench under an old tree. You are now in the Standish Park Estate, and signs on the stiles indicate this. The path goes across track and then down to another stile by a hawthorn tree. Cross this and almost immediately another stile. Continue down over grassland with fence on your left and in about 450 yards climb a stepless stile in fence on left, 50 yards from a gate in bottom left hand corner of the field. Walk straight ahead to a barn with house on left. Cross stile and go over stream, then keeping barn on your left you will come to a drive with large steel farm gate on left into farmyard. Go through this and then through another steel gate to reach the farm drive which crosses a stream before coming out onto public road.

Shortwood topograph with wide views

[C] Turn left and follow quiet road for

6

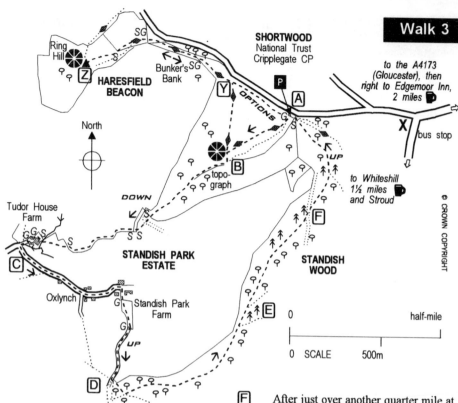

half a mile to Standish Park Farm. Go straight on past two footpaths signed to the right and first Estate notice near cottages. On entering the farmyard the footpath almost immediately turns right and is well signposted by the owner. Walk to a steel gate and then straight on up the track. Ahead are two farm gates, enter the right hand timber gate and go uphill along a tree lined path to the corner of Standish Wood.

D At the four way junction of paths turn left and for a short time follow the boundary of Standish Park Estate. Where the fence veers away to the left, continue on the steep uphill path, and in 120 yards turn left at the path junction. You now join a route which is quite wide and undulates from time to time.

E After about half a mile ignore two pathways on the right, and continue along the main track near the edge of the wood.

F After just over another quarter mile at the fork, bear right. Do not go downhill here. After a while the path rises, gently at first, later quite sharply to level out and lead to a squeeze stile in stone wall of the car park.

[OPTIONS 2 and 3 via Haresfield Beacon

A Leave car park as before, but turn right with stone wall on right and continue to metal signpost indicating Haresfield Beacon.

Y Follow the well-marked Cotswold Way downhill. Cross a stile next to a farm gate and soon after take the right hand fork uphill. Just before reaching the road the path veers to the left where there is a sign Haresfield Beacon, though the beacon proper is further on. Continue to a gate next to a stone squeeze stile, and later a timber squeeze stile. Walk to the stone trig. point now visible at **Z** and enjoy the view.

OPTION 2: Retrace your route to the car park.

OPTION 3: On return from Z turn right at Y to join the main walk at B.]

7

- **DESCRIPTION:** This 5¼ mile (8½ km) (3 hours) walk contains some steep ascents and descents. The route is varied, through woodland, fields and parkland, affording good views. The approach to Misarden Park from the lodge is regal. There is much wildlife to be seen if you go quietly.
- **OPTION 2:** 4¼ miles (7 km) (2¼ hours) - Short cut along woodland track between D and E.
- **OPTION 3:** 10½ miles (17 km) (5¾ hours of walking) - Start on either this walk or Walk 5, linking them as shown in the instructions with a pub lunch at Bisley or Miserden a possibility.
- **DIRECTIONS:** From the north, fork left from B4070 (Birdlip to Stroud) at Foston's Ash pub, left again to Whiteway, then keep straight on past Lypiatt to Sudgrove turn. From Stroud direction turn right off B4070 at crossroads signposted Miserden, over next crossroads (Calf Way), down and up, bear right twice both signed Edgeworth, to reach a right turn for Sudgrove.
- **PARK** carefully on one of the verges near this T-junction at Sudgrove turn, grid reference 938 081, OS maps Landranger 163 or Explorer 179. **BY BUS** One only, Thu, Fri, Sat from Stroud.
- **FOOD & DRINK:** Carpenters Arms, Miserden (01285 821283).

A At T-junction opposite the road signed Sudgrove go through gate to follow track across fields. After it becomes enclosed watch for path dividing in front of gate. Fork right with fence on left to go 200 yards to gateway, then after a few yards down to gate and stile. Descend right hand side of the field to corner,

P Rooke 99

Miserden tree shelter with twelve seats

where a stile gives access into wood. The path continues steeply down by fence to Ashcombe Bottom, where it turns sharp left for 250 yards to stile on right.

B Turn right over stile, and follow arrow on waymark straight up through young trees to waymark post just past them. Follow the arrow under mature trees with their trunks on your left to another waymark post. Join the bridleway track left downhill to gate. After 50 yards turn down between bungalows by Valley Farm. Turn left after bungalows, through three gates and along bank path to gate below animal shed. Just beyond gate is a 'V' stile on left, and stepping stones across River Frome.† On far side of stones go half right across damp land to reach good path and turn left (point ❷). ‡ Go on to gate. Follow green path round hill side to junction of paths near gate onto road. Ignore this and turn right steeply up eroded track to gate into wood. Continue climbing to junction of tracks, then keep beside left-

---

† *After prolonged rain the stepping stones can sometimes become submerged. There is an emergencies only alternative by permission of the landowners. Retrace steps to the first bungalow. Turn left through gate at ❻ on the map. Go half right to waymark post. Now go left down to gate. Turn right to footbridge. Cross and after a few steps go left near river bank for 200 yards to ❷. Now see‡ above.*

hand fence for gradual descent to road.

C From gate / stile opposite, ascend Bull Banks field, aiming for stile by wood. Bear left of gap between woods, over the stile aimed for into wood, climbing steeply to steps leading up to wall at top of wood. Turn left by waymark post inside wood (NOT over wall). Walk with wall on right to junction. Bear right along good path following wall to junction.

D [OPTION 2 Short cut. Bear left and follow this path along the top of the wood for nearly half a mile to a junction of tracks, where turn left downhill. Now see letter E.]
MAIN WALK Turn right into field, and after short distance beside wall on right the track veers left between open fields to Gaskill's Farm. Turn left at road, and immediately left along road to Lodge. Go through the splendid gates onto Misarden Park drive (a public bridleway). *Walking the grand Winstone Drive is a most enjoyable experience, when one can imagine a Coach and Four passing in bygone days. A backward glance just after the gates near the staddle stones affords a pleasant view of Lodge, its gates, and beyond. At right bend in drive (near gateposts), the mansion comes into view on opposite hillside.*

E Continue steeply straight ahead down track to Misarden Park lake.

Walk 4

Turn left up the park road, taking first right. Go through kissing gate by gate, and up meadow with excellent view on right of Mansion, Lake and Park. Go through kissing gate to road. Turn right to reach a slab stile. Turn right along lovely walled footpath, over another slab stile to emerge by cottages into Miserden Village. Turn left, and continue left along road past tree shelter and pub to Lypiatt crossroads. Follow Edgeworth road left for a few yards to signpost pointing right, next to a cottage, via walled path. Go through kissing gate, passing trig. point up on right and through gate into field. Cross to reach road. Notice a gate opposite. Turn left. *Do not go through this gate unless doing Option 3.*

F [OPTION 3 TO BISLEY using Walk 5. Link up by going through gate, down to stile and down steps to track, then turning right. Now see Walk 5 point D.]
MAIN WALK Follow the road back round to the start at T-junction (point A) *(see map).*

Misarden Park has many delightful permissive woodland walks, and publishes a detailed leaflet. This is available at the village shop and at the nurseries.

9

Walk 5 - 5 miles
Option - 10½ miles

Bisley, Sudgrove and Througham
Tracey Bond and Mike Garner

- **DESCRIPTION:** This 5 mile (8 km) (2¾ hours) moderate walk is across peaceful plateau-like countryside with occasional steep dives to tiny streams, and then equally steeply up again. You will be lucky to see any people, and traffic is a rarity. Througham contains some fine buildings. Bisley is a fascinating village, well worth exploring after the walk.
- **OPTION:** 10½ miles (17 km) (5¾ hours) - Start on either this walk or Walk 4, linking them as shown in the instructions with a pub lunch at either Bisley or Miserden as a possibility.
- **DIRECTIONS:** By car from the north, fork left from the B4070 (Birdlip to Stroud road) at Foston's Ash pub, aiming for Bisley. From the south and west, follow signposted route to Bisley from Stroud. From the east, turn right off the A419 road from Cirencester through Sapperton, Daneway and Waterlane to Bisley.
- **PARKING** At the five way junction by the Stirrup Cup Inn, go up tiny unnamed road directly opposite (grit box on right of junction) for 100 yards and turn into car park on left by King George playing field. Please avoid blocking side gate to adjacent house. Grid reference 906 061, OS maps Landranger 163 or Explorer 179. **BY BUS** Mon-Sat hourly service 34/35 from Stroud.
- **FOOD & DRINK:** Stirrup Cup Inn, Bisley (01452 770280), Bear Inn, Bisley (01452 770265).

[A] From car park by playing field, turn left along road for 150 yards to metal gate. Go ahead along track with wall on right past a barn until track swings left behind hedge. Here continue ahead with wall on right and descend to metal gate. Follow wall steeply down to

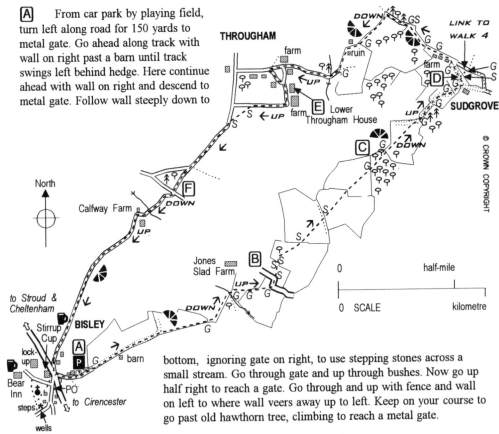

bottom, ignoring gate on right, to use stepping stones across a small stream. Go through gate and up through bushes. Now go up half right to reach a gate. Go through and up with fence and wall on left to where wall veers away up to left. Keep on your course to go past old hawthorn tree, climbing to reach a metal gate.

B Go through this gate and bear left up road for a short distance to the bend. Go ahead over stile into the field. Follow the path with a wall on the right to the corner. Cross a double stile into the next field. Bear slightly right across field passing a nearby large tree until a stile comes into view. Cross this and continue across next field towards a signpost by a wall. Go over the track and cross an old stone slab stile. Continue over two more fields in the same direction to a gate into a wood.

C Walk through the small wood and emerge through a gate. *The tiny settlement of Sudgrove is straight across the valley.* Go steeply down the meadow, aiming for a metal gate a short way up the other side. Go through the gate, *near a noisy small stream, often hidden by vegetation.* Continue uphill to go through another gate. Proceed up a wider field using track to another gateway part way up. Go through and up to pass a small barn on right. Now go up over bank to reach a gate by a signpost into a track. *This is near a large Cotswold house in a fine position.* Turn left up track away from house for 50 yards and notice steps up bank on right. *Do NOT climb the steps unless linking with Miserden Walk.* **[OPTION TO MISERDEN using Walk 4.** Link by climbing up steps, going over stile and up to gate onto road and then turning right. Now see Walk 4 point F (**MAIN WALK**).]

D **MAIN WALK.** Continue **Walk 5** up track through a gate to soon reach Sudgrove House Farm. Bear right up behind barn. Continue ahead through two metal gates. Cross meadow with wall on right to reach metal gate and wooden stile onto path with trees on right. When you reach a wall ahead, turn left downhill on clear path. *This is an old road on the maps. There are excellent views of Througham (pronounced Thruffham) over the valley.* Part way down go through metal gate. Soon pass a ruined building with excellent stonework on the left to reach another metal gate at the bottom of the hill. Go through onto enclosed track, often muddy here. Now climb up the stony track with a stream usually running down it to first turning on left. Continue up road, and turn sharply left by small garage to follow road through the delightful hamlet of Througham.

E *Lower Througham House on the left is a beautiful early 17th century gabled house with notable stone rainwater gutters and chutes. Look for the gable pigeon lofts. The .farmyard is worth a look too.* Turn right up hill looking for a footpath signpost near top on left. Cross wooden stile to go up field, aiming for signpost between two power poles close together. Cross stone stile to go left along this quiet road to a fork. Go left past woodland on the right to crossroads.

F Go steeply down (unsuitable for motor vehicles) and up the other side past a farm. Walk this pleasant road, with distant views, for about three quarters of a mile to Bisley, easy to spot with its Church spire. Emerge into the modern world by the Stirrup Cup Inn. Turn left back to car park, *although probably you will wish to explore historic . Bisley village first. Look for the lock up near The Bear Inn. In the churchyard is an open air 13th century hexagonal altar, unique in England, which was used for candles in masses said for the poor. Down the steps from the churchyard are the famous wells, dressed with flowers each Ascension Day, and at present complete with resident ducks on the water troughs.*

Bisley lock up in the village (see map)
A milestone nearby proclaims "X miles to Gloster"

- **DESCRIPTION:** A 4½ mile (7 km) (2¼ hours) mainly level walk across pasture fields and alongside the Stroudwater Canal and River Frome surrounding Eastington village. The canal sections of this walk give some indication of how busy this waterway was in the 18th and early 19th centuries, and the feats of engineering needed to make and keep it viable.
- **DIRECTIONS:** From Stroud take A419 towards the M5. Turn left towards Eastington at Chipman's Platt and immediately left into picnic site. **PARK** at Pike Lock, grid reference 785 061, OS maps Landranger 162, Pathfinder 1112 (discontinued), or less conveniently either Explorer 179 or 168 and across the join to Outdoor Leisure 14.
- **BY BUS:** From Stroud and Dursley via Eastington weekdays hourly service number 16.
- **FOOD & DRINK:** Victoria Inn (01453 822892), Kings Head Hotel (01453 822934), Little Chef on A419 at Chipman's Platt (01453 828847).

EASTINGTON VILLAGE

Only Alcrintone (Alkerton) appears in the Domesday Book as a manor. Later the Parish became Eastington and, like most villages of the Stroud valleys and Severnside, depended mainly on the woollen trade. Of its three mills two remain converted to modern use. Houses of stone or brick only proliferated after the beginning of the Industrial Revolution and the construction of the Stroudwater Canal in the early 18th Century.
Eastington Park, Eastington House and Alkerton Court have survived from this era.

At the present time Eastington has two public houses (good food), a Post Office and general store, a butcher, greengrocer, newsagent and hairdresser. For more historical details consult A History of Eastington by A S Keys 1953.

[A]   From the car park follow the towpath back past Pike Lock to Eastington Road to cross it. Take a few paces left and turn right along towpath as signed. *Note the cottages on the far bank, built originally for canal officials.* Shortly after Dock Lock turn acutely left round field boundary and follow track back to road.

[B]   Cross with care and go over stile and small field towards lych-gate. *If time allows, explore St Michael and All Angels, which has many interesting features.*

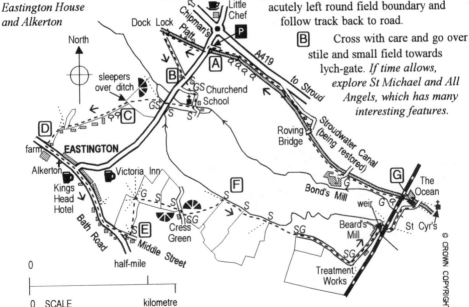

right of the well-named Cam Peak and Long Down (see Walk 11). Continue on same line to stile in corner. Go over and turn right, advancing a few paces to a signpost (you are now in Cress Green) then turn left through stile or gate. *At this point on a clear day you will see to your left May Hill, the Forest of Dean, and The Malverns. Ahead and*

Blunder Lock, Eastington, one of the restored locks on the Stroudwater Canal

Go left round church wall past postbox, then school on your left. Turn right over stile and across field with River Frome and churchyard on your right. Cross unusual metal double squeeze stile onto road again. Cross with CARE to stile or gate opposite at end of bridge parapet, into field, which is routinely cultivated. Take path diagonally uphill to top corner; the path is usually cleared by farmer.

[C]   Cross ditch on left using sleepers and go forward with trees and boundary of recent development on your left. Continue following edge of field towards ornately-roofed building ahead, which you will pass on your left 100 yards before reaching the Bath Road. *The building is a summer house built by the owner of Alkerton Grange who was much influenced by his visits to Holland.*

[D]   Cross road and turn left towards the village. Follow the Bath Road passing Methodist Chapel and King's Head on your right. *Notice attractive signpost at junction, formerly a drinking fountain.* Continue on Bath road for about 600 yards, *noting 16th Century Alkerton Farmhouse (now a private dwelling) on the right.* Fork left, as signed, into Middle Street. Proceed about 50 yards, then turn left over stile into grass field.

[E]   Take the right hand well-trodden path to top of field. Go through right hand kissing gate and take right path to go to stile visible ahead. Go over this *noticing the view to the*

slightly right is the isolated Randwick Ash on the Cotswold ridge. Descend to right hand corner of the field to willows bordering the River Frome. Aim slightly to left of large brick-built mill.

[F]   Turn right over stile near river and follow with its line of willows, crossing two more stiles in various states of repair. The path then leaves the river and in a few yards reaches a stile by gate onto a wide track which passes the water treatment works. At the end of the works cross a stile and turn left into a roughly surfaced private road. This leads to the railway viaduct at Beards Mill (note the weir on your right) where the surface improves. Go up a slight rise to join the towpath of the Stroudwater Canal at Ocean Bridge. *St Cyr's Church is visible to the right on the other side of the bridge, and you may wish to pay a visit, returning here.*

[G]   Turn left along the towpath at The Ocean *(a former busy loading basin in the days of commercial canal traffic)* and follow it back towards the car park. *By Bond's Mill is the world's first advanced composite bridge (1994). Cross to other side at Roving Bridge. Much work has been done in recent years repairing the locks on this section. You will pass Newtown Lock, Blunder Lock, re-opened by HRH the Prince of Wales in 1992, and Pike Lock. Special boating events are often held here. Note the launch slipway.*

- **DESCRIPTION:** A moderate 4 mile (6½ km) (2 hours) walk which gives a great variety of scene; fields, lanes, woodland and valley towpath of the former Thames and Severn Canal.
- **OPTION 2:** 5 miles (8 km) (2½ hours) - for those who wish for a longer route, the map indicates an extra loop of one mile from D to E including some more peaceful canal towpath.
- **DIRECTIONS:** From Stroud take the Cirencester road (A419), passing through Chalford to the top of Cowcombe Hill. **PARK** in the large lay-by on the left almost opposite Aston Down airfield, grid reference 091 019, OS maps Landranger 163 or Explorer 168. From Cirencester take the A419 to Stroud and look for the lay-by on the right just after Aston Down airfield.
- **BY BUS:** Stroud to Cirencester No 54, infrequent service, not Sundays.
- **FOOD & DRINK:** The Crown Inn, Frampton Mansell (01285 760601) or perhaps a cup of tea in the lay-by.

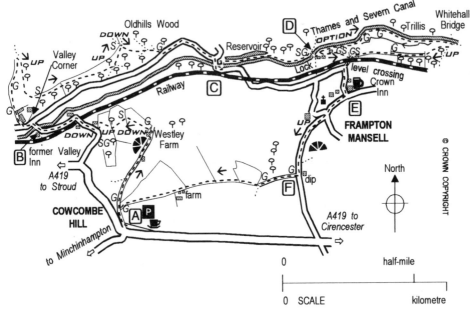

[A]   Leave the lay-by by minor road below Cowcombe Hill. Keep walking downhill passing a farm gate and cottage to reach Westley Farm. Pass farmhouse and then go between farm buildings. Turn LEFT to enter large field through five-bar farm gate. *Take time here to enjoy the wonderful panoramic view.* Descend across centre of field to the stile which soon becomes visible in the lower hedge. Cross stile and follow narrow path carefully downhill between bushes and across turf to reach a wooden double signpost. Here

turn left and follow track down and round right for a short distance, then follow track upwards keeping fence on left to top. Turn sharply left and ascend to gate / stile which can be seen at top, leading onto a road. Turn right and follow road downhill over railway bridge. *On the left, just past footpath sign, there is a fine Cotswold House, originally a Mill House. It became a pub, the Valley Inn, and is now a private house once more.*

[B]   Cross the canal bridge to the junction

and turn left. Aim for a footpath sign. Turn right at sign going between *Corner Cottage* and *Valley Cottage* and follow path to a five-bar gate. Use the chained gap and continue on track with a stream on left to another five bar gate with gap. Go by this and at the far end of the field DO NOT CROSS stepping stones to the stile on left, but turn sharp right and climb upwards on path to follow upper fence along length of field to a stile. Cross the stile into Woodland Trust property and go along footpath until a clearing is reached. Fork left uphill to another clearing with stile on left in the wall, turn right and follow path downhill, passing round a locked barrier, until the valley road is reached. Turn left and follow road to *Bakers Mill* and road bridge. Turn right across bridge and then soon take the path on left across a wooden bridge to the towpath.

[C] Turn right along towpath. *The lake on the left was created as a reservoir by the Thames and Severn Canal Company to provide water for the locks lower down where there was always the problem of seepage.* On reaching a kissing gate proceed right across a brick bridge. The towpath has now crossed to the other side of the canal. *Here is a private dwelling, once the Oak Inn, whose custom came entirely from the canal folk. After years of dereliction, it has now happily been restored.* Walk for a few yards to a junction of paths just beyond second house.

[D] [OPTION 2: (5 miles) Continue left for half a mile along towpath (rather like a nature reserve), through two kissing gates, until you reach the brick built Whitehall Bridge. Turn right here and soon right again (by manhole cover). Follow muddy path to gate into field. Ignore gates on left, and cross field to

reach level crossing.]

MAIN WALK (4 miles) At D the main route now leaves the towpath. Turn right at junction (private drive ahead). Bear left upwards on a wide track going by a farm gate over a two step stile. Ascend the wide grassy track and pass through a stile / gate at top. [OPTION 2 rejoins MAIN WALK] TAKE CARE going over the level crossing and proceed up the road (ignore right hand turn). Here there are attractive Cotswold houses and gardens and soon the Crown Inn will be reached on the left.

[E] Turn right following pathway. Note the attractive model railway layout in the garden of *Church Cottage* on the right just before bus shelter. *The tower of the neo-Norman church of St Luke built in 1844 may be glimpsed next below.* The walk continues going gently up alongside white railings and then along edge of road (take care). Continue upwards out of village, eventually reaching a dip in road with bridleway sign on the right.

[F] Follow bridleway for three quarters of a mile, passing a group of farm buildings, eventually reaching a five bar gate leading onto the road followed at the commencement of the walk. Turn left uphill to the lay-by.

The Golden Valley with Frampton Mansell Church in the foreground

15

- **DESCRIPTION:** This moderate / hilly 7 mile (11 km) (3½ hours) walk passes through parts of 4 National Trust commons. The paths have exceptional views over the Woodchester and Golden Valleys. Starting in the historic small Cotswold town of Minchinhampton, you might allow time to visit the 11th /14th century church and the Market House (1698). The Lord of the Manor's tariff is displayed on the wall. The walk continues through the pretty village of Box, across Minchinhampton Common, skirting Pinfarthings and Amberley to Rodborough Common. Then progress is made above the Golden Valley through Bownham and Besbury Commons via picturesque hamlets steeped in history from the area's flourishing woollen industry times.

- **DIRECTIONS:** From Stroud, Minchinhampton is signposted off the A419 Cirencester or the A46 Bath Road. There is a free car park and various street parking in the town. Start the walk at Minchinhampton Market House, grid reference 872 007, OS maps Landranger 162 or Explorer 168. **ALTERNATIVE START** National Trust car park near Winstones Ices on Rodborough Common, grid reference 855 029 (letter D).

- **BY BUS:** Several daily Stroud 28/29/54, Cirencester 54, Nailsworth 28/62, Tetbury 29, not Sun.

- **FOOD & DRINK:** *Minchinhampton,* Crown Inn (01453 882357), Coffee Bean (closed Sundays, Mondays and half day Saturday, do check times) (01453 883382), Sophie's Restaurant (01453 885188), *Box,* Halfway House (01453 832631), *Amberley,* The Amberley Inn (01453 872565).

[A] From Market House go down to cross roads. Turn left into Tetbury Street. After post office turn right into Chapel Lane. Take footpath on right past *Field House* over stile. Hug wall on right to bottom. Ignoring stile on right turn left along field edge then over stile on right. Carry on down between two fences to stile by gate. Continue down field to metal gate, over a bridge, through another metal gate then half left past lake to top left corner. Cross stile onto road, turn left then bear off right up past *Gardener's Cottage* on left to T-junction. Turn right uphill and soon left on walled path and through kissing gate. Carry on with wall

Rose Cottage

on left. Pass through another kissing gate in stone wall. Continue on round field edge to further kissing gate and yet another (four in all) to track.

[B] Turn right to road then left into Box passing church with gold spire on left. Bear left down side road. Bear right along level road to junction. Turn left and at telephone box cross to go along right edge of village green and in corner take walled path. At road turn left up hill. In 20 yards left up onto Minchinhampton Common, crossing track and fork of two roads. Carry on straight ahead across common keeping golf course on right and parallel to road on left for half a mile. Go under power line. In 100 yards come down to road next to power pole. Bear right along road. At fork bear left to pass *Rose Cottage (where Mrs Craik was staying when she wrote 'John Halifax Gentleman').* Go right 10 yards along next drive, then bear left onto grass path. This leads through gap. Bear right with hawthorn tree and power pole on right to graveyard wall. Go left down to road and turn right. At *Maddock Land* follow wall and hedge on left. Follow path downhill. At top of road take uphill

16

path right to main road. Turn left and in 100 yards turn right up track to reach *Barns Close*. Now turn left, keeping wall on right to carry on down to road. Turn right and at road junction continue on upper road signposted St Chloe. At next junction turn left into wood at footpath sign.

[C] Follow path and at fork in about 200 yards drop down to lower path. After another 200 yards cross track by stone bridge and continue for a mile with views over Woodchester Valley. Just short of iron fence turn right uphill to go through gate. Continue with wall on left to road. Turn right, go up for 100 yards. Cross cattle grid to take path by

National Trust sign steeply up to Rodborough Common. At

top turn right and continue with wall on left to road (Bear Hotel on right). Fork left at top to cross road by public byway sign and follow this to Winstones Ices.

[D] **[ALTERNATIVE START]** At left side of building follow winding path down with hedge on right. When track appears, carry on down through gate to reach road. Turn right and after 200 yards go right 60 yards up side road and through gate, up track through wood to reach road. Turn left on top road with wall on right across Bownham Common. Ignore right fork by dew pond. After another 300 yards at junction by *Roseland* go straight on down past *1 Jacobs Knoll* and steeply downhill. Where road veers right at *Hollies* step up bank on right 10 yards after *Sweetbriar*. Follow level path past double power poles, overlooking the valley and through the hamlet of Claycombe to join road. Continue steeply up to main road.

[E] Turn right uphill and go first left into Burleigh Lane. Follow for 500 yards to grass triangle. Keep left by *Burleigh House* on right. Then bear right past *Burleigh Farm* on left. Later at second triangle keep left. When road starts to descend take right path over Besbury Common

keeping on higher path. Pass two stone stiles and soon turn right through stile with iron posts to enclosed path. Go over stile, cross road and over stone stile. Cross paddock to go over next stile and bear right up road. At crossroads go right to The Great Park. Bear left skirting the houses. Go through iron gate left into churchyard and keep by wall on right. Go through lych-gate. Turn left into Minchinhampton.

Rodborough Common
STEEPLY UP
North
Bear Hotel
CG
P D
DOWN
UP
UP
Bownham Common
small dew pond
1 Jacobs Knoll
Roseland
Hollies
Sweetbriar
DOWN
Claycombe
E
BURLEIGH
Besbury Common
iron posts
The Great Park
C
St Chloe
DOWN Amberley Inn
© CROWN COPYRIGHT
Maddock Land
Rose Cottage
power line
MINCHINHAMPTON
Centre
Market House
Tetbury St
Field House
Minchinhampton Common
FB
SG
PINFARTHINGS
Half Way House Inn
BOX
Forwood
DOWN
0   half-mile
School
lake
0 SCALE   kilometre
village green
B

17

Walk 9 - 7½ miles
Options - 3 & 14½ miles
Minchinhampton, Hampton Fields, Cherington Pond, Aston Down - Ruth Cook

- **DESCRIPTION:** This moderate walk 7½ mile (12 km) (3¾ hours) goes over Minchinhampton Golf Course with beautiful views and alongside pretty Cherington Pond. It is good for seeing birds and flowers. It returns by more level route to Minchinhampton, an interesting small town.
- **OPTION 2:** A moderate 3 mile (5 km) (1½ hours) walk - from Hampton Fields (points BCDB).
- **OPTION 3:** A moderate / hilly 14½ mile walk (23 km) (7½ hours of walking) - Walks 8 and 9.
- **DIRECTIONS:** Minchinhampton is well signposted. **PARK** in free car park in town, or alongside wall-enclosed allotments on Tetbury Road, grid reference 874 005, OS maps Landranger 162 & 163 or Explorer 168. **ALTERNATIVE AND OPTION 2 START** Hampton Fields (point B). Take Tetbury Road from Minchinhampton for 1½ miles. Bear left and go over crossroads to fork right onto road to Nag's Head. **PARK** on long grassy verge on right, grid reference 886 996.
- **BY BUS:** From Stroud, Cirencester, Nailsworth, Tetbury, see Walk 8.
- **FOOD & DRINK:** *Minchinhampton*, Crown Inn, (01453 882357), Coffee Bean (check times) (01453 883382), Sophie's Restaurant (01453 885188), *Avening*, Cross Inn (01453 832953).

[A] Walk away from centre towards Tetbury. Immediately after cattle grid take track on right. This soon becomes an enclosed path leading to a stile. Go over and down steep hill towards track on hill ahead. Go over stile by gate at valley bottom and climb up track, past another stile with gate and later bearing right. Soon after you come to a junction at which turn left onto tarmac farm road. Stay on this until the main road is reached where route turns right. *To see The Long Stone cross road and look slightly left in the field. The Long Stone is perhaps the most famous Gloucestershire megalith. It was thought in past times that if children were passed through the hole in the stone they would be cured of rickets and smallpox. There is a second stone built into the wall on the left of the first stone. These may be part of a long barrow.* Continue on this busy road, passing The Lodge and private drive to Gatcombe Park on right and complex road junction.

[B] **[ALTERNATIVE AND OPTION 2 START** From car walk back to junction to do three left turns to join Tetbury Road.]
MAIN WALK Continue along road signed to Tetbury for 400 yards to

Unusual wall stile near Avening

footpath sign on left. Go over stile in wall and follow direction of sign to slab stile in wall. Continue with wall on right to another slab stile. This brings you onto Golf Course (waymarked path). Watching for stray shots, follow across to pass club house and car park. Keep beech hedge on left until it curves to left, then bear right on earth path. As track bends right continue straight on with hedge on right. Just after green keepers' sheds, at *Norn's Tump*, go through hedge and follow right of two mown grass paths to gap in wall (waymark). Continue to stile just visible in fence. Go down steep hill to unusual stile on wall.

[C] *(Cross Inn, Avening 600 yards right)* Turn LEFT onto road and continue past houses in Nag's Head. Later ignore footpath going up left. Soon after reaching bridge go through gate on left to path which goes beside picturesque Cherington Pond. *The pond area is famed for its wonderful display of snowdrops. The pond is home to Mallard, Coot, Moorhen, Swan and Little Grebe, and in summer with other birds, feeding on*

18

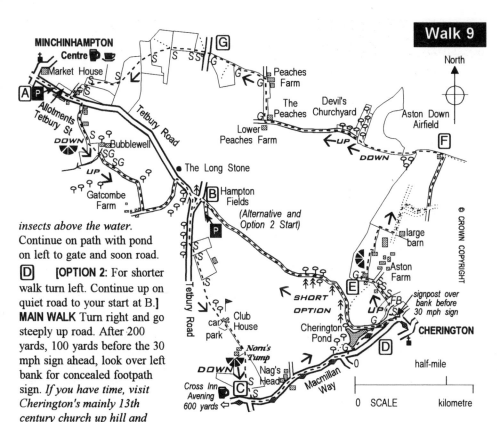

insects above the water.
Continue on path with pond
on left to gate and soon road.

D **[OPTION 2:** For shorter
walk turn left. Continue up on
quiet road to your start at B.]
MAIN WALK Turn right and go
steeply up road. After 200
yards, 100 yards before the 30
mph sign ahead, look over left
bank for concealed footpath
sign. *If you have time, visit
Cherington's mainly 13th
century church up hill and
return here.* Go over stile and downhill to
cross stile and footbridge and then up steep
hill with fence on left. Follow path with wall
on left over two stiles to driveway.

E Turn left at minor road and in about
100 yards look for waymark post on left and
follow its direction through gate on right into
field. Keep wall on right to another waymark
post and continue with hedge on right to end
of field. Turn right towards barn and follow
hedge on right to junction. Turn left along
track. Bear right at waymark post onto track
and continue to footpath signpost. Turn left
(not waymarked) onto enclosed track.

F At path junction turn left by airfield.
Continue on track, passing wooded *Devil's
Churchyard* at bottom of slope on right. *All
trace has gone of large "holey stones" in the
Churchyard, thought to be connected with the
Old Religion practised before Christianity.
Later a new Church was started on the pagan*

*site but this was destroyed (attributed to the
Devil).* Turn right through narrow gate at first
house on right. *(The Peaches).* Go up narrow
field to go through gate. After 50 yards near
houses turn left through gap in wall before
gate ahead. Follow wall on right of field. Go
through gate and second field to reach road.

G Cross road and go over stile and follow
path with wall / barn on left. Go over slab stile
through field. Go over another slab stile. Bear
slightly left on left hand path of two to stile in
wall. Now follow path to wide gap in hedge
line and then diagonally across field (using
stone post with white top as guide) and over
slab and timber stiles. Continue with wall on
right. In 150 yards (where broken wall on right
forms junction at right angles to path) bear
diagonally left and using white topped posts as
guide to stile in wall. Follow waymark to two
stiles into farmyard and onto road. Bear left to
the start. Minchinhampton Centre is to right.

19

Walk 10 - 4 miles
Options - 2 and 6 miles

Stinchcombe Hill, Stinchcombe and Stancombe - Mervyn and Pansy Allen

- **DESCRIPTION:** A moderate / hilly but rewarding 4 mile (6½ km) (2½ hours) walk which has magnificent views over the Severn Vale to the Forest of Dean. The upper limestone grassland of Stinchcombe Hill supports 11 species of orchid amongst its varied flora attracting a recorded 31 species of butterfly. The walk follows the escarpment around the Hill, and then drops steeply down through woods and fields to Stinchcombe Church. After a stroll through Stinchcombe village it climbs through meadows, where there are wonderful vistas. Finally it passes Stancombe Park to climb following the Cotswold Way back up to the car park on the Hill.

- **OPTION 2:** Easy 2 mile (3 km) (1 hour) stroll around top of Stinchcombe Hill (points ABEA).

- **OPTION 3:** Moderate / hilly 6 mile (9½ km) (3½ hours) walk. Add the level stroll to main route.

- **DIRECTIONS:** From Dursley traffic lights by post office go off A4135 along May Lane. Turn right by Old Spot Inn along Hill Road / Broadway to top of hill. Turn right to **PARK** at the large public car park on Stinchcombe Hill near the far end of the narrow road across golf course on left, grid reference 744 984, OS maps Landranger 162 or Explorer 167. **Alternatively** park in free car park opposite Old Spot Inn, Dursley, and take route as described below from bus station.

- **BY BUS:** From Stroud 15/16, Gloucester 91, Bristol 309, Mon-Sat hourly to May Lane bus station, Dursley. Walk Cotswold Way up Hill Road, entering wood at signpost, taking middle path beyond chain up to Club House, then along road to A. This adds about a mile to each walk.

- **FOOD & DRINK:** The Old Spot Inn, Dursley (01453 542870).

[A] **MAIN WALK & OPTION 2** From the public car park face the vale, turn right, and after 100 yards drop down bank to follow Cotswold Way waymark. After 400 yards climb up through a few trees and turn left for 20 yards to a fine promontory viewpoint. About turn and continue round side of hill to climb through trees. Turn left for a few yards to Drakestone Point. Turn round again and bear left towards the Sir Stanley Tubbs Memorial Seat. *The undulating ground here is due to ancient fortifications.* Follow path to left of the trig. point. *You won't see New York and Paris indicated on the nearby*

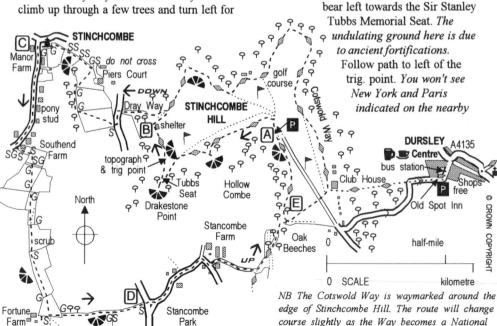

NB The Cotswold Way is waymarked around the edge of Stinchcombe Hill. The route will change course slightly as the Way becomes a National Trail. It should continue to be clearly signed.

© CROWN COPYRIGHT

20

topograph, but on a clear day you should see the Sugar Loaf and Brecon Beacons across the Severn Vale. Go on to a stone shelter.

☐B☐ **[OPTION 2** Continue clockwise around the hilltop following Cotswold Way waymarks (see page 32) and cut across hilltop by Club House to circle back to car.]
MAIN WALK Follow path for 100 yards. BE READY to go sharply left down a track in the woods. After 50 yards bear right to drop down a steep path off the track. In 15 yards pass a confirming waymark post. Continue steeply downhill on the path *(The Dray Way)* ignoring side paths to the B4060 road. Cross the road CAREFULLY and turn left to a signpost and stile on the right. Go over stile and diagonally right to far corner. Go into a small wood through a kissing gate and continue with fence on right to another kissing gate. Now cross field heading towards drive left of *Piers Court, former home of Evelyn Waugh.* At stile / gate onto drive DO NOT cross but turn acutely left back up across field keeping higher wood on left to reach a double stile. *Here the spire of Stinchcombe Church is seen, with the Severn Vale beyond making a fine view marred only by the buildings of Sharpness Docks and the sudden roar of the M5 which will accompany you for some way.* Continue down to church crossing two small fields. Enter churchyard through gate. *The church is well worth a visit.* The footpath leads down to the left, and out at the lower end by a fountain in the wall. Across the road is Manor Farm.

☐C☐ Go left through Stinchcombe on level quiet road, past cottages and ponies. Reach Southend Farm on left after half a mile.

Go on to footpath sign and through gate on left onto farm

Walk 10

drive. Cross stile and go across small paddock to further stile. Cross and go right to metal gate and stile. Next head slightly left up to a meeting of four fences. Go through gate on left and immediately a gate ahead into higher field. Now go on level path on right to a gate. In the next field go through scrub to cross stile. *In this field views gradually widen across Waterley Bottom, North Nibley, the Tyndale Monument ahead, and even both Severn Bridges.* Cross field to gate to enter field with farm over to right. Cross the field to stile in hedge. DO NOT climb but turn left up to gate. Carry on uphill now with hedge and trees on left. Continue up over stile by gate and on to stile to road.

☐D☐ Cross main road with great CARE and follow minor road opposite signposted Stancombe with *Stancombe Park Gardens* behind wall on right. Keep going past post box to fork in road. Here go right to pass front of Stancombe Farm. Go up track on left between farm and a house. Go steeply up en-closed track to meet Cotswold Way coming in from right. Continue left up in woodland. Turn right near top to open grassland on hill.

☐E☐ **[OPTION 3:** If you wish to walk another two delightful miles, continue straight ahead across the hill top on the Cotswold Way to go in front of the Golf Clubhouse for a complete anticlockwise circuit of this beautiful hill and arrive at car park from the opposite direction.]
MAIN WALK Follow path left through a copse then enjoy more views from hillside for over a quarter of a mile before reaching car park.

The Tubbs Memorial Seat near Drakestone Point

Walk 11 - 7½ miles
Option - 3¾ miles

Cam Peak, Uley Bury, Coaley Peak, Far Green and Cam Long Down - Charles Hartley

- **DESCRIPTION:** This hilly walk of 7½ miles (12 km) (4½ hours) affords panoramic views of the Severn Vale to the Forest of Dean and the Brecon Beacons, goes round Uley Bury, the finest hill fort in Gloucestershire, through beechwoods of the Cotswold edge to Coaley Peak (764 feet, 233 m) with another fine view, plunges down to the valley below through charming meadows in Far Green, wends its way by delightful lakes stocked with ducks and geese and finishes by climbing up Cam Long Down, isolated remnant of the Cotswolds with Oolitic Limestone cap.
- **OPTION 2:** A shorter but still hilly walk of 3¾ miles (6 km) (2¼ hours) (ABCGA).
- **DIRECTIONS:** Turn east in Dursley off A4135 down Kingshill Lane, up Church Road, right up Springhill Lane. **PARK** at top of rise, on right, at foot of Cam Peak, grid ref. 767 994. OS maps Landranger 162 or Explorer 167. **ALTERNATIVE START** Coaley Peak (B4066), grid ref. 794 014.
- **BY BUS:** Service 15 Stroud / Dursley to Nympsfield, Mon-Sat 1-3 journeys. Walk from D.
- **FOOD & DRINK:** The Rose & Crown, Nympsfield, (01453 860240).

[A]   Leave car park by interpretation board to climb to saddle between Cam Peak and Long Down. *Perhaps detour to Peak, with a fine view of Cam. There is an annual pilgrimage here as an act of Witness on Good Friday, carrying a Cross from Dursley and leaving it on the Peak over Easter.* Continue over saddle. Bear left down to paths junction. **CHOICE of 2 routes to B from here. 1. MUDDY bridleway in places.** Bear right downhill. Soon a gate leads into track. *Banks of primroses and bluebells in season.* Fork right down drive. At bridge go forward gently uphill on sunken bridleway to road at B. **NB 150** *yards of mud likely near top.* **OR 2. DRIER footpath / quiet road.** Turn right down to level path by fence. Go right; soon cross stile on left. Down field with hedge on left to stile. Left up road for half mile to point B.

[B]   At Hydegate go to junction by kennels to take bridleway ahead, and fork right at entrance to garden. After 50 yards, leave on footpath to left up steep bank. Pass over stile. Climb diagonally past posts, way-marks on top. *Views of Tyndale Monument, Downham Hill, Cam Peak, Long Down, and in the*

Alternative Start
Coaley Peak [P]
Picnic Site [E]
STEEPLY DOWN
Ham Farm
FB
Far
Green
Farm
[F]
North

B4066
to Stroud   Entrance to Woodchester
Park (NT)
(waymarked walks)
NYMPSFIELD

SHORT CUT

Hetty Pegler's Tump (access from road only)

Rose & Crown [D]

© CROWN COPYRIGHT

0   half-mile

0   SCALE   kilometre

Cotswold Way
lakes
FB
Cotswold Way

Long Barrow

OPTIONS TO LINK WITH WALK 12 HERE [C]

[A]
[P]
DOWN Cam Long Down ←UP
saddle
MUDDY IN PLACES
Cam
Peak
often bridge v.muddy up here

Hodgecombe Farm [G]

STEEPLY UP

Uley Bury

to Dursley and Cam
2. DRIER ROUTE
Hydegate [B]
Downham Hill (no rights of way)

distance May Hill and the Malverns. Cross stile and take path to left. A further stile brings you onto track around Uley Bury. Turn right. *The steep climb gave us the opportunity to reflect on the defensive situation of Uley Bury iron age*

22

P. Rooke 99

Panoramic views from Uley Bury

camp. *It would have been a nearly hopeless task to attack up this hill and brave defenders behind wooden fences on top of mounds. The 32 acres are now cropped - no access. Enjoy fine views of Uley and Owlpen. Springs part way down the limestone hills feed the Ewelme River in this valley and powered many woollen mills, now cottages of character.* Pass through twin poles to track towards road on right. Bypass gate, go left by second gate to junction.

C **[OPTION 2:** If you wish to do a shorter walk, take Cotswold Way to your LEFT, down to bottom of hill, past Hodgecombe Farm and turn right to rejoin main walk at point G. Return over Cam Long Down to point A.]

MAIN WALK Take Cotswold Way going down to your RIGHT. Fork right off track almost immediately onto footpath and enter woods. Skirt some interesting limestone cliffs. *The well maintained footpath passes through Woodland Trust beech woods. Look out for owl pellets; little bundles of fur and bones regurgitated by owls. Naturalists find these are important indications of diet.* At junction, fork right gently up at first then more level. At next junction, take right fork to climb steeply up through Coaley Woods. Meet B4066 Dursley to Stroud Road at top of hill. **[SHORT CUT** to point E - go carefully downhill on road for 90 yards, then follow Cotswold Way right]. **MAIN WALK** Cross road. Follow signs to Nympsfield.

D There is an opportunity here to take a meal at the Rose and Crown in the pretty village of Nympsfield. Return taking the first left uphill from the Inn and soon pass through gate into field on right. Cross two fields with stiles and cross the busy B4066 CAREFULLY. Walk a short distance right on verge and follow path down to magnificent viewpoint on Coaley Peak, also known as Frocester Hill.

E **[ALTERNATIVE START AT COALEY PEAK PICNIC SITE** - walk to topograph]. After taking in the views from AA topograph CAREFULLY follow very steep path directly downhill to road. Go right for a few yards then continue down path to next road. Turn right and go down a short distance. Turn left down bridleway. After 50 yards by tall stone wall, enter field on right through gate. Cross field with copse on your left and make for gate ahead at bottom of hill. Pass through gate, where stream flows under through culvert. Enter Ham farmyard through gate and turn left before barn to road. Turn right, then left at road junction for about 150 yards to footpath sign. Follow right over field, with a concrete pad on your right. Go over stream and through gate. Turn right along hedge to footbridge but do NOT cross. Turn sharp left across same field AWAY from bridge, towards left of distant houses, then over stile. Cross field on same line to stile right of brick house.

F In Far Green turn left past bus stop a short distance to crossroads. Turn right and almost immediately leave road to left on path through gate. Walk up hill skirting wood on right. Cross stile *(note recycled plastic fence posts)* and continue to skirt the beech wood. Follow a terrace down into valley, past house up on left. Cross side stream by elevated footbridge and walk up enchanting valley by a series of lakes, with ducks and geese. Keep a house high on your left and pass through first farm gate onto road. Turn right to pass farm.

G Rejoin Cotswold Way, turning right over stile. Pass over two stiles steeply up onto Cam Long Down and along its length, back to the saddle. Cross and walk down to car park.

23

Walk 12 - 5 miles	Owlpen, Uley and Uley Bury
Options - 12½ and 8¾ miles	Kathy Bullen

- **DESCRIPTION:** A fairly hilly 5 mile (8 km) (3 hours) walk looking at Uley from all angles, and particularly rewarding in Spring when the daffodils are in bloom. Allow at least three hours for the walk, as you will wish to linger in many places. The walk goes round Uley Bury, the finest hill fort in Gloucestershire. It is lovely in Summer for its limestone flora and Marbled White butterflies. Owlpen Manor is reserved for the end. It dates from about 1400 and has one of the oldest mediaeval gardens in existence. Uley was a centre of the woollen industry, making Uley Blue cloth, The village has some fine houses, although all the mills have closed. Several mill buildings are visited, and the millponds for these are wildlife havens, so take some bread to feed the ducks (if the fish don't get there first!).
- **OPTION 2:** A hilly 12½ mile (20 km) (7 hours) walk, combine walk with all of Walk 11.
- **OPTION 3:** A hilly 8¾ mile (14 km) (4½ hours) walk, combine walk with Walk 11, option 2.
- **DIRECTIONS:** From B4066 Stroud to Dursley road take Fiery Lane east from Uley Village Green. In ½ mile go down round sharp corner. **PARK** either side, near post box, grid ref. 799 984. OS maps Landranger 162 or Explorer 167 / 168. **ALTERNATIVE START** Uley Church (B).
- **BUS** to Uley village green from Stroud / Dursley No 16 hourly Mon-Sat. Walk from point B.
- **FOOD & DRINK:** Old Crown Inn, Uley (01453 860502).

[A] Continue along road for a few yards. Cross first stile to right of gate, noting stile on opposite side of road where the walk finishes. Follow stream and cross stile in facing hedge. *The millpond on your right has a variety of waterfowl and you may see tits, woodpeckers and the occasional heron and even kingfisher.* Turn right at end of pond then immediately

A view of Owlpen Manor and Church in the early Spring

cross field half left to stile in bottom hedge. Cross stream by stepping stones and follow right-hand path up field towards housing estate, where a stile under a large tree leads to path between hedges. This path emerges onto Uley Village Green, a delight at all times but particularly when the daffodils are flowering. The Old Crown Inn is on your left. Cross main road to Uley Church.

[B] **[ALTERNATIVE START]** Take path immediately behind Uley churchyard. Turn right up enclosed path to kissing gate. Climb field to top left-hand corner (not visible at first), where gate leads into wood. Path goes up forward and slightly right to leave wood by a stile. Go steeply up to emerge on perimeter track of Uley Bury. Bear right and at end turn sharp left over cattle grid, embedded in mud.

[C] *This 32 acre hill fort (see map) has never been excavated. You will realise its size and commanding position as you walk round three sides of it.* Along this path soon you will be able to appreciate the view. *On a clear day the Severn Vale, the Malverns and the Welsh hills may be seen, with Cam*

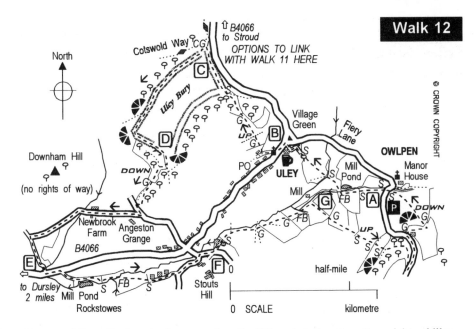

Long Down and Cam Peak in the foreground. Downham Hill with its visible track and group of trees on top is known as Smallpox Hill. It was to an isolation hospital on top that sailors suffering from smallpox were brought from Sharpness Docks. As you turn the second corner, Dursley and Cam come into view. AT THIRD CORNER CLIMB SECOND GRASSY KNOLL AHEAD.

D Here you may obtain an excellent view of Uley. Then take the stony path down from this knoll. In 40 yards, as you bear right, note your path which goes into the wood ahead - slightly left of the Tyndale Monument on the skyline. Take left hand track after gate to lead you down to the road. Turn left and almost immediately right by tall stone wall, along a bridleway. Later pass farm, going below Downham Hill. At T-junction turn left to road.

E Go left up pavement to its end, cross carefully and take track opposite. Bear left at mill buildings, and the path takes you ahead past overgrown millpond in trees on right. A stile leads into a field. Follow stream to cross footbridge on right. Aim left towards buildings to cross a stile. This leads to track behind them and takes you on to road. Turn left along road

for 300 yards to junction. Turn right uphill to to Stouts Hill entrance. *This was once a school (noteworthy Old Boys being Mark Phillips and Stephen Fry) and is now a time-share.*

F Take path opposite Stouts Hill and follow path ahead to keep another beautiful mill on left. A stile leads into field. You may glimpse its millpond behind left hedge. Follow hedge and go ahead to metal kissing gate into next field. The path leads to another kissing gate, then downhill to hidden footbridge. Keep to left hedge in field until crossing fence (do not cross), noting large mill building on left - once powered by water in pond seen earlier.

G Turn right along fence and go through first gate in facing hedge. Cross stile in top left of field, another straight above and yet another into wood. *You may wish to sit on the bench to take in the panorama from here.* Take track left through wood, to emerge onto Fiery Lane. Go downhill and take gate on right immediately past houses. Go on level across to gate in left hedge. Go through and aim for the church tower across middle of field. The magnificent view of Owlpen Manor and church in its delightful wooded valley opens up. Continue to stile in bottom left to finish.

25

Wotton-under-Edge, Laycombe Wood, Ridings Wood and Coombe Hill - David and Margaret Woodall

- **DESCRIPTION:** This moderate 6 mile (9½ km) (3 hours) walk takes a circular route northwards along the Cotswold escarpment from Wotton-under-Edge. The outward section is mainly through isolated mixed woodland including permissive paths by courtesy of the Woodland Trust. In the Springtime there is an abundance of wild flowers to be enjoyed along these tracks. The return journey mainly through pastureland affords extensive views across the Severn Vale to the river and, on a clear day, to the Welsh Mountains. The walk concludes with an opportunity to enjoy views over the hamlet of Coombe, and the ancient town of Wotton-under-Edge with a vast panorama towards Bristol and the River Severn.
- **DIRECTIONS:** By car, park in the Civic Centre car park in Gloucester Street, Wotton-under-Edge, grid reference 756 934, OS maps Landranger 162 or Explorer 167.
- **BY BUS:** Dursley 15/309, Bristol 309, Stroud 15/40, Gloucester, Yate 621/623, not Sundays.
- **FOOD & DRINK:** Royal Oak, Wotton (01453 842316) and a choice of cafes.

[A] Leave Civic Centre car park by turning right down Gloucester Street but immediately turn left to climb Tabernacle Pitch passing the picturesque *Rowland Hill's Almshouses* on right. Tabernacle Road then climbs steeply and leads to well-used path continuing upwards between high hedges to Old London Road. Here turn right but take the opportunity to catch your breath and enjoy the scene from the viewpoint. Briefly continue climbing along road to reach stile on right leading into Conygre Wood. On left the path leads past Scouts' camp site with adjacent Gloucestershire Wildlife Trust Nature Reserve. Continue through woods to reach kissing gate with steps down into Adey's Lane.

[B] Turn left up the road but almost immediately turn right at T-junction along Old London Road passing dilapidated barn on left. On reaching signpost turn left down road signed to Waterley Bottoms. Go downhill for 400 yards to a gate with stile on right leading into Laycombe Wood. Immediately a second gate is reached bearing Woodland Trust notice. Continue forward along track climbing gradually and passing a barrier with stile. Within a few yards a junction is reached with a well-worn bridleway. Turn left downhill and pass a blue waymark.

[C] After 60 yards leave the downhill track and turn right along permissive bridleway. This path is likely to be muddy in patches. On the left there may be rewarding glimpses, particularly in winter, across the valley to Westridge Wood. The path follows an undulating route generally close by upper edge of Laycombe Wood. After three quarters of a mile, near gate with *private* notice, Upper Rushmire Farm may be visible through fringe of trees on right. The Ridings Guest House with tall trees near is higher up. Continue along well-worn path ignoring several lesser paths leading down. Springs discharge across path here so muddy stretches can be expected most of the year. After another three quarters of a mile, views on left across Waterley Bottom reveal glimpses of Tyndale's Monument and the Severn Vale. Keep to higher path into Ridings Wood, noting two isolated cottages hidden in woods on right. The path skirts gardens with a waymark indicating route ahead. Climb to arrive at stile into the open.

[D] On crossing stile head diagonally left on the indistinct public footpath over a long unsurfaced drive, climbing slightly past large tree on left towards small fenced copse in middle of field. Pass copse on your left to reach a stile and gate. Climb stile into small thicket, and scramble upwards to emerge into open field. Immediately turn right and proceed southward keeping copse on right. Look for a stile at hedge corner slightly up on left. Cross and follow field boundary on right. At end of

stile near house and follow stepped path to Adey's Lane. Turn left down road but immediately right through kissing gate and follow the path behind gardens. After crossing minor road follow footpath (surfaced) to emerge alongside former Tabernacle Church. Go down Tabernacle Pitch to Gloucester Street with car park opposite on the right.

Rowland Hill's Almshouses with former Tabernacle Church behind

field take time to enjoy views across to Tyndale's Monument on Nibley Knoll, Westridge Wood and the River Severn. The Ridings Guest House with its tall trees nearby will again come into view higher up the hillside. On climbing further stile, continue with field hedge on right and drop down to gap in pointed corner of field. Bear left up across next field to stile by signpost in hedge onto the Old London Road.

[E] CAREFULLY cross and turn right along the single track road, making use of the wide verges to avoid occasional but fast moving vehicles. Continue ahead to a group of barns (Bradley Barn). Turn left onto bridleway signposted to Coombe. Follow track until it begins to drop more steeply and a stile is reached on the right. Cross into open pastureland of Coombe Hill and note the view over the hamlet of Coombe. Continue around hill and absorb the extensive southerly aspect over Wotton-under-Edge, Bristol and beyond.

[F] The path arrives at a gate with adjoining metal stile. On crossing stile a clear track leads into mixed woodland. After 150 yards take path sharply left then after 100 yards bear right to drop down to

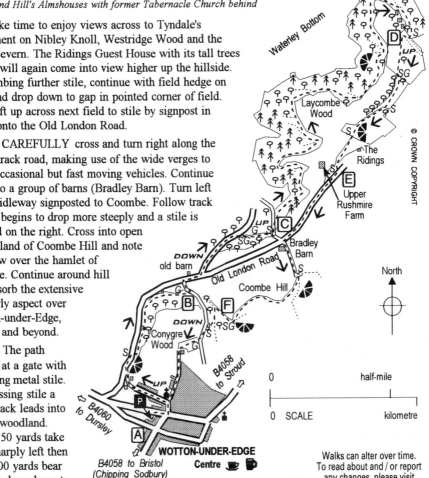

© CROWN COPYRIGHT

Walks can alter over time. To read about and / or report any changes, please visit our BOOKS UPDATE PAGE at www.southcotswoldramblers.org.uk

- **DESCRIPTION:** This fairly easy 5½ mile (9 km) (2¾ hours) walk from the historic village of Beverston surprises with its panoramic views. It goes through a deep valley to Longtree Bottom, with carpets of bluebells in season, and later visits Chavenage. Watch out for resident hare, buzzard and badger. Linger in Beverston before the walk to see Norman towered church - noting pre-conquest sculptured figure of Christ on the south face. The castle, also pre-conquest, the residence of the Berkeley family from 1154 - 1597; besieged and captured from the Royalists in the Civil War, and now enfolding the private farm residence within its walls.

- **OPTION 2:** Easy 3 mile (5 km) (1½ hours) *'just one stile'* walk visiting Chavenage (ABEFA).

- **DIRECTIONS:** By car from A46 (Stroud-Bath), turn onto the A4135 towards Tetbury. After 1½ miles turn left in Beverston village (turning after the one with sign "to Norman Church"). From east take A4135 (Dursley Road) off the Tetbury-Cirencester road. After 1½ miles turn first right in Beverston 100 yards BEFORE red telephone box and proceed past castle gate to church.

- **PARK** sensitively between Beverston Church and field gate, allowing vehicular access, grid reference 862 940, OS maps Landranger 162 or Explorer 168.

- **BY BUS:** Nailsworth circular Monday, Tetbury circular Wednesday & Friday, information 01452 425543.

- **FOOD & DRINK:** Gumstool Inn (01666 890391) (see map), or several places in Tetbury.

A   Enter field west of Church by cattle grid or gate. Turn right following wall on right to lone tree. Continue with fence / hedge on your left to gate / stile and follow the same line across grassland down to the corner.

Beverston Castle

B   [OPTION 2 - 3 miles. Go through metal gate on right. Continue up on occasionally muddy path with trees then hedge on left to bridleway sign at *Chavenage Green Cottages*. Turn right. Now see point E.]

MAIN WALK After arriving at point B take wooden gate on left. Go across field to mid-point of hedge (prominent ash tree). Here keep tree and overgrown pond on left to go through gap in wall (white post). Bear left across next field to white post at mid-point of hedge. Go through gap to continue on same line heading to right of nearer conifers and buildings. Go over stone stile at signpost, cross road and go over stile into field towards left corner (pine trees). Ignore metal gates on left and go over stile on left shortly before end of field to cross plantation to stone stile. Turn right onto farm road and follow past cattle grid and gates to woodland in dip.

C   Turn right along valley, keeping woods on left for 500 yards to gate. Gate areas can be muddy, and this is worse than most. Continue to keep to woodland edge to metal gate ahead. Bear right towards other side of next field, but keep LEFT of fenced off bog / pond area to reach opening on right (waymark).

Cross stone dam / bridge, go through gate and turn left. Cross field aiming for house on horizon. Pass hidden Ledgemore Pond below on left. When distant house disappears from view veer right around hill towards stile / gate in wall ahead. Go past small pump house - *housing a fine 'Lister's of Dursley' pump* - into woodland.

D   Follow track along bottom of bluebell wood, listening for warblers and nuthatch - path can get badly cut up but plenty of width to pick your way. After half a mile pass through small birch plantation and under power line into field. Continue with boundary on left to signpost at gate / stile. Bear slightly left across small field to pole gate onto road at *Chavenage Green Cottages* and turn left.

E   Go along road with its magnificent avenue of lime trees to farm on right. Continue on main road for 200 yards to *Chavenage House*. View the front of the house through the gateway. *This historic Elizabethan house was once the residence of Colonel Nathaniel Stephens who was visited by Oliver Cromwell. He was persuaded to put his name to the death warrant for the execution of King Charles I. Apparently he was full of remorse later and died three months afterwards. An open air theatre production now takes place annually in the grounds. The house is open Thursday and Sunday afternoons, May to September.* Retrace your route for 200 yards and turn left (signpost opposite) to pass fine Elizabethan barn on left. Follow often muddy Chavenage Lane, part of the Macmillan Way. Pass through two gates near bottom. Bear left then right with boundary on right to climb to gate. *Look back here for good view of Chavenage House.* This higher level gives an extensive vista to Tetbury's church spire, over the Vale of Malmesbury and beyond, and to the west a good view of Beverston.

F   Turn right at signpost **Walk 14** onto verge of A4135 road.
Be alert for speeding traffic and hidden drainage ditches across verge. Thankfully after 350 yards the village pavement is reached. Turn right by *Forge House* into tranquillity. Go along 'no through road' across green to barn, a fine 14th century building, and on to Church to finish the walk.

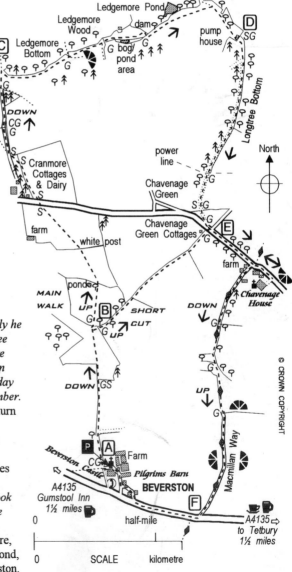

29

- **DESCRIPTION:** This moderate to hilly 5 mile walk (8 km) (2½ hours) follows the Cotswold Way from Wortley through Alderley, then diverts onto lesser-used paths through a lovely part of the Cotswolds. A fine track leads up a beautiful valley to the hilltop village of Tresham. The route drops down hillside into Ozleworth Bottom, with excellent views, and returns to Wortley.
- **DIRECTIONS:** <u>By car from the north,</u> take the minor road south from the War Memorial roundabout at Wotton-under-Edge, signposted to Alderley and Hillesley, to reach Wortley. <u>From the south,</u> turn left off the A46 at Dunkirk, just north of the Petty France Hotel and follow the minor road NW to Hawkesbury Upton,Hillesley, Alderley and Wortley. <u>At Wortley</u> turn east and go 100 yards up a road signposted to Ozleworth.
- **PARK** on a wide verge on the right. Please do not block the entrance to Elmtree Farm. Grid reference 767 916, OS maps Landranger 162, Explorer 167.
- **BUS:** Wotton to Wortley by Yate service Nos 623 or 627; several daily, not Sundays.
- **FOOD & DRINK:** Fleece Inn, Hillesley (01453 843189) or several places in Wotton-under-Edge.

[A] The Cotswold Way crosses the road beside the parking place. Go over stile on south side, turn half left and walk diagonally down large field. *In the valley is a fish farm based at an old woollen mill. The pure, limey Cotswold water suits many such farms.* Cross stile in far corner of field, then another in 50 yards. Bear right up track called Kennawell Lane. *This is a corruption of St. Kenelm's Well, a mediaeval spring, much visited then for its curative properties. The spring can be seen on left, 100 yards up track; a four foot high waterfall in winter, it dries up in hot summers.* At top of track, join road and turn right for 30 yards to crossroads. Go straight across and follow road (Cotswold Way); *in 100 yards look for ornate gateway on left. This was built 150 years ago, and leads the eye up Winner Hill to a castellated folly, recently renovated, but not accessible.* Continue ahead past old mounting block to road junction; Alderley Church is on the right.

[B] Turn left then left again in 15 yards at bridleway signpost along Cotswold Way. Follow drive between buildings; it deteriorates into a track. There is a gate after 100 yards and another after a further 100 yards. Look out for

views of the Winner Hill folly on the left. A third gate is 50 yards on. The track then follows the bottom of large field to a stile by a gate. Continue 50 yards down sunken track,then go through second gate on the right, leaving Cotswold Way. Follow grass track ahead as it swings left to approach Newmills Farm. By barn, go through gate, then over stile right of building. Aim just left of farm up hillside, left of fence, to stile. Then follow fence for 30 yards and continue in same direction when fence veers right. *To the right are the extensive*

Alderley, gateway leading to the folly on Winner Hill

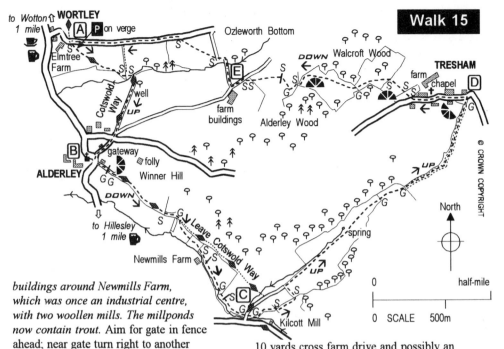

to Wotton⇧ **WORTLEY**
1 mile
A P on verge
Ozleworth Bottom

Elmtree Farm
well UP
Cotswold Way
DOWN Walcroft Wood
farm chapel TRESHAM
E
farm buildings
Alderley Wood

B gateway
folly
ALDERLEY G G
Winner Hill
DOWN
to Hillesley 1 mile
Leave Cotswold Way
Newmills Farm
C
Kilcott Mill

North

© CROWN COPYRIGHT

spring
UP

0   half-mile

0   SCALE   500m

buildings around Newmills Farm, which was once an industrial centre, with two woollen mills. The millponds now contain trout. Aim for gate in fence ahead; near gate turn right to another gate, then down a grass track to follow stream to stile by gate. Go ahead to follow stream and fence to gate onto well named muddy track, Water Lane.

C   Our route, however, avoids the mud. Go through gate opposite, then diagonally left up field, noting Kilcott Mill to right. Aim for large fence corner post then follow fence up to stile. Beyond this, turn left *(note views right up the Kilcott valley)* along hedge to stile on left near corner. Go left down fence for 100 yards to join track and turn right up valley. *Note how the stream on left comes from a very powerful spring.* Just beyond this is a gate. Continue up valley to right hand of two gates opposite small barn. Go on up sunken track. At fork, bear left by fence. *On the right is a steep hillside, covered with "sheep walks," which are caused by "soil creep", emphasised by the sheep.* After gate by wall, it is 75 yards up to the road at Tresham, a hilltop village.

D   Turn left, passing a small bench from which there is a fine view down the valley. Pass the Victorian chapel on right. Just beyond last buildings on right cross a stone stile. After 10 yards cross farm drive and possibly an electric fence. *Half right is the modern Ozleworth TV and radio relay tower. Left of this, on the skyline, is a large house, Newark Park (National Trust).* Aiming to left of Newark Park, cross field until stile comes into view. Go steeply down beyond this, then half left to marker post in hedge gap. Steeply down again then turn half left to pass right of pond to gate. Turn right down middle of next field to reach another stile. *From this there are fine views of Newark Park, Ozleworth Bottom and the Severn Valley.* Cross stile, turn left down by fence and through wood to small gate. Turn left and veer right around head of small valley to isolated stile, which once stood in a fence. Go half left down field to stile by metal trough. In another 50 yards a stile leads onto track. Turn left towards farm buildings.

E   Just before farm, turn right down concrete track. Cross stream *(stones of another old mill on either side)* and swing left. In 50 yards, turn left over stile, then turn half right and cross field to stile onto quiet road. Turn left along road and the parking place is just half a mile away.

31

ACKNOWLEDGEMENTS

This book is the result of much meticulous research by many people, and the thorough checking and invaluable suggestions of others. Without their willing help, enthusiasm and teamwork, production of this book would not have been possible. I have attempted to name them all here, an activity not without risk, but if anyone has been missed out, you know who you are! I am very grateful to all members and friends who have helped in any way, including Mervyn and Pansy Allen, Lorraine and Martin Arnold, John Bond, Tracey Bond, Ron Bowring, Mike Brinkworth, Kathy Bullen, Audrey and Tom Capper, Ruth Cook, Gloria Crocombe, Karen and Tony D'Amico, Tony Drake, Anne Eamer, Heather Garner, Olivia Gunn, Charles Hartley, Margaret and Peter Heaton, Doug and Joan Hobbs, Anne Hull, Pat Hutton, Chris and Margaret Judson, Brian Kirkman, Joyce Longhurst, John and Margaret McArdell, Cynthia and Don McKie, Ann and Michael Poole, Norman Pullen, Jacqui Pycroft, Bob and Mavis Rear, Jack Redfern, Molly and Norman Roberts, Peter and Sondra Rooke, Anne Sinclaire and Brian Woosey, David and Pam Smith, Lin and Peter Tanswell, Margaret Taylor, Alan White, Betty and Harold Wood, David and Margaret Woodall, John Workman OBE and Frank Wragg.

I would also like to acknowledge the help and advice of the staff of the Gloucestershire County Council Public Rights of Way Unit, printer Barry Hathaway, distributor Nicholas Reardon, The National Trust, The Woodland Trust and many other landowners and farmers. MG June 1999.

FACT FILE

⊃ **THE COTSWOLD WAY** NB this is being transformed into a National Trail over five years. Always well-waymarked with white spots next to yellow (footpath), blue (bridleway) or white (road) arrows, National Trail acorns will be appearing and minor changes will be occurring.

⊃ **PRACTICAL POINTS** Comfortable walking boots are always a good idea for walks in this area. Also useful is a small day sack with waterproofs, a sweatshirt (usually cooler on hill tops), a snack and drink (usually welcome part-way around walk) and a simple first aid kit.

⊃ **PUBLIC TRANSPORT** Apart from service 46, Stroud - Cheltenham, no buses run on Sundays. We give you an idea of frequency on each walk, but for up to date bus timetable details ring the County Public Transport Helpline (01452 425543) M-F 8-5. Other numbers: Stroud Bus Station, (01453 763421), Gloucester Bus Station (01452 527516), Stagecoach, Cheltenham (01242 522021). Rail information - National Rail Enquiry Line (0345 484950).

⊃ **TOURIST INFORMATION CENTRES** Stroud Subscription Rooms, George Street (01453 765768), and information points at Nailsworth, Fountain Street (01453 832532), Painswick Library (01452 813552) and Wotton Heritage Centre, The Chipping (01453 521541).

⊃ **PATH PROBLEMS** If a path is planted you may walk its line through the crop. If the line of the path is dangerous, you should find a way round. When looking for alternatives, you may have to trespass, which is not a criminal offence. Be careful not to cause damage as under civil law you might be liable for damages. **PLEASE** take the time to report any problems to the *Public Rights of Way Unit, Gloucestershire County Council, Shire Hall, Gloucester GL1 2TH*, giving if possible full details, location, sketch plan, where path runs to / from and a grid reference. Do contact South Cotswold Ramblers c/o RA, London if in doubt.

⊃ **THE RAMBLERS' ASSOCIATION** (RA) works for all who appreciate walking. Many members of the RA enjoy meeting other people on regular walks, social events and holidays. Some volunteer to keep an eye on rights of way and make comments on countryside changes. Please contact RA, London (0207-339 8501) (address at front) for the benefits of membership.